Employed
for Life!

Employed for Life!

AN INSIDER'S SECRETS FOR GUARANTEED EMPLOYMENT IN OUR PERMANENTLY CHANGED WORKPLACE

P. Anthony Burnham, Esq.

SelectBooks, Inc.

This edition published by SelectBooks, Inc. For information, address SelectBooks, Inc., New York, New York.

First Paperback Edition

First hardbound edition published in 2004 by SelectBooks, Inc.

Paperback edition ISBN 978-1-59079-185-1

The Library of Congress has catalogued the original hardbound edition as follows:

Library of Congress Cataloging-in-Publication Data

Burnham, P. Anthony, 1942–
    Employed for life! : an insider's secrets for guaranteed employment in our permanently changed workplace / P. Anthony Burnham. -- 1st ed.
    p. cm.
ISBN 1-59079-058-8 (alk. paper)
    1. Vocational guidance. 2. Vocational qualifications.
    3. Performance. 4. Self-presentation. 5. Self-culture.
    6. Career development. 7. Job security. I. Title.
HF5381.B779   2004   650.1--dc22
2003024079

To Gail, my beloved and eternal partner,
whose unconditional love and support
have helped me to discover
my own value,
which has enabled me to pursue
my personal and professional mission.

CONTENTS

Becoming an 'employer of results' sounds easy.
It isn't.
It necessitates giving incompetence
nowhere to hide.
It requires managing by using the simplicity
that exists on the far side of complexity.

—P. ANTHONY BURNHAM

FOREWORD

It's a typical day at one of the nation's corporations. The boardroom is crowded with highly paid executives with worried looks on their well-groomed faces. Hit by the devastating impact of the dot-com implosion, the recession, the attacks of September 11, ever-increasing foreign competition, and now the endless accounting scandals and resulting plunge in stock prices, the CEO declares "it's time for yet another 'reduction in force', another round of layoffs."

This time the reduction in force will affect many loyal employees with over twenty years of experience, many of whom are approaching retirement. The pink slips will also be flowing freely to other highly paid employees holding positions no one ever dreamed would be at risk. In fact, although they don't know it yet, some of the people in the boardroom won't be at their own big desks either come Monday morning.

At the very same time, several floors below the paneled boardroom, in a much more modest conference room a select group of board members and key executives are having an emergency meeting, also called at the direction of the CEO. The purpose of this meeting? To discuss the number-one challenge to the company's survival: how to attract and retain enough productive people in key positions throughout the company to meet the increasing demands of its customers and fend off its competitors.

What's up with that? How can a company possibly be ending the careers of loyal employees (with twenty-plus years of experience, no less!) while at the same time scrambling to attract and retain "good people"? Welcome to the *paradox* that increasingly defines today's (and tomorrow's) workplace!

Today's workplace is forcing companies of all sizes and descriptions to *permanently and significantly:* 1) reduce costs and, 2) increase productivity. For you, this means that seniority or past achievements can't save your job if you don't produce more, better and for less *right now.* To put it plainly: *Yesterday's job security is gone and it's never coming back!*

The workplace has become incredibly challenging both for employees competing for their livelihoods and businesses competing for their profits. At the same time, also paradoxically, it is a workplace that has unparalleled promise for you if you learn to take full advantage of your permanent "temporariness"; and for businesses, if they learn how to attract, retain and manage "free agents", like you, who know their Value.

So what are the new "rules of the road" that will lead you and the progressive companies you chose to work with to new levels of success in the 21st century? In this permanently changed "bizscape", do you and smart employers have anything in common that you can build on together for your lasting, mutual benefit? The answer is a clear and resounding—*Yes!*

Today, you and the businesses you want to work with share a common need—namely, to produce more, better, faster and cheaper *results*. For you, producing *more results* leads you to what *you need*—greater *work security,* now and in your future. For the progressive businesses you choose to work with, employing people like yourself who produce *more results* leads them to what *they need*—greater *competitiveness* and *profits*. This common need to continuously produce better results *unites* you with, rather than divides you from, the businesses to which you want to contribute. Now that's a foundation worth building upon, and it's about time. But how do you and your future employers jointly discover and then build upon that foundation?

For that, you will need to read this book very carefully. It involves a journey during which you will learn how to determine your own Value, how to develop it and how to continuously and effectively communicate it. If future employers want to survive by competing for your services, smart CEOs and key managers will read this book to learn how to attract and keep you in their organizations.

This book was written by a 35-year veteran of the courtroom and boardroom who, because of his considerable success in bringing workers and management together, has a clear understanding of how you and any business smart enough to lure you to them can enjoy a *win-win* relationship based upon long-term mutual productivity.

The following pages give you a rare opportunity to learn the unvarnished truth from an insider who has "been there and done that," an insider who is willing to help you achieve a lifetime of employability—*starting right now!*

Employed for Life!

The art of progress is to preserve order amid change, and to preserve change amid order.

—ALFRED NORTH WHITEHEAD

ONE

The Workplace:
My, How You've Changed

What a difference a couple of decades makes. Up through the 1940s, '50s and even '60s, the whole idea of earning a living seemed a lot simpler: you got a job with a good-sized company, collected your paychecks and built up your pension benefits for 20 years, then retired to a life of regular golf games, lawn care and maybe building model ships in your garage. You were secure in your longevity with the company, feeling—rightly or wrongly—that your loyalty was returned in kind by your supervisors and the company.

But things have changed radically since those days. Employees today expect to spend only 2 or 3 years, if that long, with each employer before moving on. But what most employers won't tell you is that today, despite greater accountability and productivity from their employees, they generally offer what amounts to

3

only temporary work. Competitiveness requires flexibility on the company's part, so employees are expected to be equally flexible: you may not realize it but, in most cases, you are being hired for the duration of a specific project or for a specified period of time. In the past, people knew their careers might include one or two terms of temporary unemployment; now you should be prepared to be employed only temporarily. In fact, though they may not tell you so, some employers today may regard 20 years with the same company as an indication that you may be too "entitlement-minded" or unable to deal successfully with the project-based assignments that are mainly available.

The olden-days manager controlled the means (namely *you*) and the means controlled the ends (the results). Today's managers control the ends (the results), and the means (again, *you*) control the way the ends are achieved. In large part, you are expected to manage yourself. Today you are selected on the basis of demonstrated self-reliance and a proven track record of contributing results, and hired—not with thoughts of a 20-year relationship—but rather for "as long as this works for both of us." You also can expect to be "reselected" or "deselected" at least annually by virtue of your performance, which is measured not in loyalty or longevity, but in *results*.

Being a successful manager in today's world means helping you to lead yourself and providing you with the resources and support you need to accomplish your agreed-upon and well-defined objectives. Successful leaders of the new millennium are more "empowering" than all-powerful. They share information, establish a broad direction, set performance criteria and then let those responsible get the job done. These leaders facilitate and coach. They rely on their competence, not mere authority, to reach their goals, and they expect others to do the same. They view success as an ongoing process rather than a single event. There is great opportunity in these changes for you and your work security.

Even with the uncertainties about tenure and self-direction, the outlook for workers ready to embrace the new reality in their careers—and for their employers—has never been brighter. Although job security may seem to have vanished completely, in fact it has shifted from being something dictated by an employer to something controlled by you. The new rules say that *you* control your employability rather than rely on a false sense of security offered by the organization that employs you.

By understanding the changes that have taken place, you can begin to gain greater control of your own future. The answers to virtually all of your uncertainties lie within yourself. You must know what you bring to the table—you must understand your own value and be able to communicate and demonstrate it on demand.

By coming to terms with your individual value and then continually striving to increase your own worth to the organizations you serve, you can find the only true "job security", and it is far more substantial and gratifying than anything past generations experienced. The security you seek will then come from your own confidence in your abilities, skills and knowledge—your Value (with a capital V). Just as facing your own mortality causes you to want to live a full life, accepting the reality that your working life will likely include several employers rather than just one causes you to take personal responsibility for shaping a fulfilling career.

CASE STUDY: BOB'S STORY

The Secrets of Self-*Empowerment*

A few years ago, Bob, the manager of a mid-sized manufacturing firm, was involved in a performance improvement project. Bob was asked to observe three work groups—high performers, average performers and poor performers—with regard to their behavior, attitude, skills and knowledge.

The study's goals were to identify differences among the groups, devise a plan to raise overall performance levels and bring average and poor performers closer to their high-performing peers.

The results were fascinating. Bob was surprised to find no noticeable behavioral differences between the three groups. The only variation was in the workers' responses to the question, "What is keeping you from performing at a higher level?"

- The high performers indicated fewer than three perceived reasons that they couldn't perform at an even higher level.

- The average performers identified six perceived reasons that they couldn't perform at a higher level.

- The poor performers cited 12 or more perceived reasons why they couldn't perform at a higher level.

Since the reasons were admittedly more perceptual than real, Bob realized the performance differences were probably related to the employees' views of their own power and their own ability to remove the blocks to higher level performance. That is, the differences lie in what employees *thought* were blocks to better performance, rather than in *actual* blocks. Further testing reinforced Bob's conclusions.

The employees' perceptions fell into four categories:

1. **Real Blocks to Higher Performance**

   Perceived higher-performance blocks that were in fact real included factors over which the employees truly had no control. This category includes items such as the state of the national economy, competition, the international exchange rate, the company's organizational structure, funding, processes, etc. These are all very real blocks for the employee and although they're not unalterable, changes in these areas come from outside or external forces much larger than mere individual desire to change them.

2. **Assistance and Support Blocks To Higher Performance**

   These are blocks to higher performance that the employees can remove or modify, but need assistance to do so. These blocks can be managed and removed through team effort, more time, financing, additional personnel and/or other resources. Eliminating these blocks generally requires upper management support and involvement.

3. **"Old Belief" Blocks to Higher Performance**

   Often there are perceptions within an organization

that appear to be truths only until they are tested. Once they're tested and proven wrong, there is a paradigm shift—a major change in perception—in the old belief system. This is quite a phenomenon and generally requires a team of employees to collectively support the idea of testing the "old ways." These belief blocks include: "The boss won't approve;" "Other departments won't support it;" "It's policy;" or "But this is the way we've *always* done it;" etc. Doing things differently is often required in order to lift old-belief blocks.

That last sentence may sound like a Catch-22—you have to do things differently in order to lift the old-belief blocks, but you have to lift the old-belief blocks before you can do things differently—and in a sense, it is. Change is usually resisted, but it *can* happen if an individual or group leads it, and that person or group must be encouraged by being rewarded for initiating it. Once the initial hurdle is overcome, change is more acceptable. It requires two leaps of faith: one by the employer to support innovative thinking on the part of the work force, and one on the employee's part to accept the incentive. Greater possibilities exist for those kinds of changes today because the talent/employees are responsible for the results, and employers are starting to recognize that. This is Opportunity (with a capital O), and workers can take credit for being agents of change.

4. "I Can't" Blocks to Higher Performance

This mindset is often more apparent in the below-average performers and is extremely hard for management to overcome. Individuals are in control of how they act, or do not act, due to how they perceive themselves. Often, when people say "I can't," what they're really saying is, "I'm afraid to." It's frightening to take action, to take a risk that's based on your own thoughts and ideas. It's much easier to stay safely inside the "I can't" fence and complain about how things are than it is to take action to try and change them.

Coaching, support and communication can help these individuals ease their fears, but it can be a lengthy and often frustrating experience for management.

Group Self-Empowerment Exercise

Once he'd absorbed the results from this performance improvement project, Bob decided to involve all three groups in a self-empowerment exercise to help reshape their thinking and generate new, alternate behaviors.

Bob assembled the three groups and encouraged employees to identify, out loud, in front of everyone, any blocks they viewed as obstructing productivity within the company. He assured them there were no "wrong" comments, that everything would be fairly considered and that there would be no retribution for speaking frankly. Each identified block was written on a board verbatim so as not to change the meaning, control or "edit" the speaker.

Once the list was complete, several blocks had been identified. Bob then asked the group to attach a value to each of the blocks, using a scale of 1 (most serious) to 5 (least serious). As it turned out, the group considered most of the blocks to be 3s and 4s. When a 1 or 2 was suggested, many of the top-performing employees offered constructive suggestions about how to overcome it.

What Bob found was that the exercise helped the average and poor performers feel they had a say in what went on within the company, which helped boost their sense of value and knock down some of their perceived blocks to higher performance. The exercise also brought a sense of teamwork to the employees that led to more interaction and less resistance to suggestions from peers about how to improve.

Before he ended the meeting, Bob made sure that all employees understood that these exercises were part of a continuing process to help each employee better manage their own performance and improve their performance for their own sakes, as well as to benefit their employer.

The good news for all of us is that the economic opportunity that has been synonymous with America for over 100 years is not gone, it's just found in a different place that where our parents, teachers and supervisors taught us to look. In today's business world it is not seniority and stability that are rewarded, because those alone do not contribute value to an organization. It is your individual contributions to measurable results that create value, and for such performance you will be rewarded with compensation, recognition and career stability far in excess of that of any generation past.

Despite our loss of market share to global competition, the economic ups and downs of the recent past and even horrific acts of terrorism, the United states remains the world's strongest economy. We are a giant, rich with natural resources, and we have tremendous wealth, military power, entrepreneurship, innovation and world influence. Our knowledge-based workplace has been dosed with steroids by our continuing developments in information technology. Our standard of living is still the highest in the industrialized world. We enjoy low inflation and relatively low taxation. We are politically stable.

World's Top 5 Economies Ranked by Real GNP-2002 (est.)

United States—-$10.4 Trillion
Japan—-$3.55 Trillion
Germany—-$2.184 Trillion
France—-$1.54 Trillion
United Kingdom—-$1.52 Trillion

Source: Central Intelligence Agency, *The World Factbook* 2003.

America is, as it has always been, a nation with heart and spirit, filled with free and imaginative people who have their roots firmly imbedded in entrepreneurship. We are an energetic, creative and resourceful bunch. We are more prepared to deal successfully with all of the transition in the workplace (and elsewhere) than perhaps we realize. For us, the challenge of adapting to change is mainly one of preparation and attitude, *not ability.*

• • • • •

The misery of uncertainty is worse
than the certainty of misery

—VICTOR FRANKL

A Study in Contrasts:
Workplace Changes—Past, Present & Future

Past/Present	Present/Future
National	Global
Tactical	Strategic
Short-term thinking	Long-term thinking
Manager as "Player"/Controller	Manager as "Coach"/Facilitator
Directive	Participative
Militaristic	Philosophical
"Bottom-line"	Balanced results
Means/Ends	Ends only
Information "taker"	Information "giver"
Learned	Intuitive
Powerful	Empowering
Source	Resource
Hierarchy	"Virtuality"
Top-down	Bottom-up
Rigid	Flexible
Cynical	Trusting
Order	Structured "chaos"
Formal	Informal
"Ass-kicker"	Praiser
"Pusher"	"Puller"

Past/Present	Present/Future
Authority	Competence
What's wrong	What's right
Lose/Win	Win/Win
Cold/Detached	Warm/Involved
Judgmental	Fair/Supportive
Management	Self-management
Subjective Accountability	Objective Accountability
Complexity	Planned simplicity
Uniformity	Diversity
Equal	Relevant differences
Answers	Questions
Process-driven	Values-driven
Rules	Ethics
Proud	Humble
Self-centered	Centered-self
Training	Selection
Development	Self-development
Managers vs. workforce (Us vs. Them)	Managers support workforce (Us)
"Outside-in"	"Inside-out"
"Work"	"Fun"
Employed	Self-employed
Temporarily unemployed	Employed temporarily

The Permanently Changed Workplace: Major Characteristics

1. "Knowledge" Work Available

Knowledge + Results = Employment Security

Knowledge is power—Acquire, build and retain power/control

Acquiring knowledge is a continuous process, not a one-time event.

2. Self-Employing

Each person is his/her own business.

What are we selling? To whom? How?

Multiple employers—Mainly "project"-based work

Performance—Self-measured against specific, agreed-upon objectives

3. "Empowered" Workplaces

Managers as supportive coaches, not bosses— "I am my own boss!"

Organizations—Achievement/performance, not merely seniority-based

Working community-based capitalism; interdependent "whole" resulting from independent "parts."

Strong links = Strong chain

4. Work, Not Jobs

Employment, like knowledge, is a continuous process, not a single event.

Not, "Did I do my job today?" but rather "Did I achieve the results needed today?"

Jobs—Too narrow/inflexible ("event"-oriented)

Work—Broader, more needs-focused ("process"-oriented)

Chapter 1: Checkpoints For Learning

- Today, you are hired and retained on the basis of your demonstrated self-reliance and your proven track record of contributing results.

- Successful leaders of the new millennium are more "empowering" than powerful—they rely on their own competence rather than mere authority to get the job done, and they expect you to do the same.

- Work security has shifted from being something dictated by an employer to something largely controlled by you. "At will" employment has become a two-way street. Properly self-managed, your side of that street will provide you a long and successful career.

- You must understand your own Value and be able to communicate and demonstrate your worth on demand. Facing the reality that you, and not others, are responsible for your life and career sets you free to take greater responsibility for shaping your own future.

- By understanding the scope and types of changes that have occurred in the workplace, you can take full advantage of the opportunities available to you through knowledge that, by performing, you can control your own work security and career.

• • • • •

Our national roots are firmly embedded in entrepreneurship. It won the West, and then the free world. Capitalism works as well for individuals as it does for businesses.

At the heart of the free market system is the individual who is prepared to make a continuous contribution to his/her own business, to someone else's, or to both.

—P. ANTHONY BURNHAM

TWO

First Steps

Now here is the good news that most employers won't tell you: *all of the insight you need to thrive in today's changed workplace is entirely learnable and, like riding a bicycle, once learned, you'll never forget it.* Developing the required insight involves a shift in self-perception more than anything else. Seeing yourself as a "product" or "business" that you continually market, both between "jobs" and while actively employed, is the self-view that can and must be acquired.

Both today and in the future, being hired and retained depends on the specific results you contribute, not merely your regular attendance, positive attitude or formal education. It is the value found in the application of your skills, as well as how you market that value, that will determine your success in the newly competitive workplace. And it is through your recognition of the value you contribute, and actively finding ways to contribute more, that your work security will be guaranteed regardless of what changes take place either in a particular business that you are providing your services to, or in the economy generally.

The bottom line is that you must prepare yourself in fundamentally different ways to create and control your career security in today's workplace. You must focus on "work", not "jobs". Doing the work required is what is needed, not just doing "your job". Because of their narrowness, "jobs" too will soon be relics of the past. Good riddance! Whatever security "jobs" may have offered in the past, is now being far outweighed by their limitations on your opportunities to learn and use new skills by making broader contributions "outside the box".

So How Do *You* Change *Your* Perspective?

First and most important, you must see yourself as your own individual "business", and then mind your own business by thinking, acting and performing accordingly. Having the skills to consistently produce required results, in myriad working environments, is the only way that your "business" can succeed. It is the only real security available to you, and it is far more real than the mirage-like "job security" of past generations.

To succeed, you need to know exactly what your basic skills are, and likewise, you must be conscious of your weaknesses. You need to recognize what actions you have taken to demonstrate those skills, and what quantified results have been produced as a result of those actions. You must apply business and marketing concepts to both seeing and selling yourself as the product.

For most of us, such concepts are new in the context of employment—this is not the way you were taught to think about or see your career. The need for you to know about the features and benefits of the goods and services that you buy or invest in is well accepted. You understand that companies must communicate or market their products' features and benefits to you in order to get you to pay for those products or services. But to have to continuously market *yourself*, as an individual, through your achievements, to your employers is a very different matter. It is a new paradigm—a new way for you to think.

"But what about my degree?" you ask. "Don't my past contributions secure my future? What about seniority? Is there *anything* I'm entitled to?"

The answers to those questions are brutal:

- Yes, it's good that you have a degree; congratulations. The degree can be the key that gets you through the door of employment—but your actions and results are what will keep you employed.

- No, your past contributions don't secure your future, but they can help secure your continued employment.

- Your seniority alone carries little weight, but having a lot of experience at producing results carries a lot.

- And no, there really isn't anything you're *entitled* to, but there are things you can continue to *earn* and get credit for being able to do.

These days employers can afford to invest only in people who consistently produce results for them. Global competition will not allow anything else. A new game has begun, and only the strongest will survive. Your educational background, past experience or even skills alone won't sell your "product". Your features and benefits, in the form of results that you have and will consistently attain, will.

In this regard, people with more work experience and, therefore, more contributions to results have a clear advantage over those with shorter work histories. Would you rather buy from an experienced business or one that has yet to prove itself? So seniority does have some value in today's workplace. But that value stems from service that has contributed more results over time, not just from the length of time employed at any one place. The calendar alone means little, but measurable contributions over time, are of great value.

You must accept the fact that your employment security is your own responsibility, not your employer's. Producing measurable results frees you from ever feeling "fired"—that is, useless, worthless, unwanted. If your contributions are no longer needed by a particular employer, then you take them where the need exists. When no employer needs you, you must develop or enhance our skills—you must add to your individual value. The significant difference is that *you,* not *they,* are truly in control.

Keeping your current skills up to date, along with acquiring new ones that produce the results you sell, is the process you must become comfortable with if you are to be continuously investment-worthy and thus "employed". In that process, your old career dependence on your employer is shed and your new career independence (defined as "depending on yourself") is acquired. Acquiring and developing your skills, applying them in ways that produce specific results, and then selling those results to employers who will in turn provide you the opportunity to further build your inventory of skills and results will, in the new millennium, bring a happy end to the very concept of "unemployment" forever.

Broadly viewed, there is really nothing "new" about the changed workplace. In truth, we have merely returned to basics. After all, didn't free enterprise begin with the need for each of us to continuously bring value to the marketplace? Of course it did. But in today's workplace the value you bring will not be found anywhere but inside yourself. You must market that value to current or potential buyers (employers), so the first step is to be able to identify it and then communicate it to others.

The dirty little secret is that the opportunity has always been here for all of us. It is more than the American dream; it is the new American reality that you can not only participate in, but that you can control.

The way to be safe is never to be secure.

—BENJAMIN FRANKLIN

KEY QUALITIES OF A "DEPENDENT"/REACTIVE WORKFORCE

1. Managers are weary from having to do their own and others' work.
2. Most work involves "putting out fires". Work is focused more on activity than results.
3. Employees have become "entitled" to their employment, paychecks and increases.
4. The results/reward relationship is minimal or nonexistent.
5. When sales increase, profits decrease or remain flat.
6. Work has been divided into too many specialized "jobs".
7. Employees don't connect either their own work or that of others to the overall success of the organization.
8. At day's end, more problems than solutions have been identified.
9. Wasting of company time and materials is often ignored.
10. Motivation to achieve comes from outside, not inside, most employees.
11. Positive energy is reserved for weekend activities, rather than being used at work.
12. Career development is seen as the responsibility of the company, not of each employee.

CEO's Perspective:
"Our people aren't results-focused because they really haven't had to be. Times have changed. Now they do."

KEY QUALITIES OF AN "INDEPENDENT"/SELF-RELIANT WORKFORCE

1. You are responsible for doing your own "job" and other "work" that needs doing.
2. Work is focused on achieving well planned, well defined results.
3. Employment and compensation are linked to results.
4. The results/reward relationship is a well-celebrated core value of the organization.
5. When sales increase, so do profits.
6. Work is distributed into fewer "jobs."
7. You "own" your work, and are willing to collaborate with coworkers to accomplish the results needed by them.
8. You take personal responsibility for both preventing and resolving challenges.
9. Company time and materials are highly valued by you because you feel "ownership" in the parts as well as the whole organization.
10. Your motivation to achieve comes from inside, not outside, you.
11. Positive energy is both used and acquired by you at work as well as on weekends.
12. You are responsible for developing your own career. The company supports that growth based on specific contributions that you make.

CEO's Perspective:
"Sure, it's tough being the leader of so many chiefs. But these days, no business can afford to be staffed otherwise."

Chapter 2: Checkpoints for Learning

- All of the insight you need to thrive in today's changed workplace is entirely learnable and, like riding a bicycle, once learned, you'll never forget it.

- Both today and in the future, being hired and retained depends on the specific results you contribute, not merely your regular attendance, positive attitude or formal education.

- Whatever security "jobs" may have offered in the past is now being far outweighed by their limitations on your opportunities to learn and use new skills by making broader contributions "outside the box".

- To succeed, you need to know exactly what your basic skills are, and likewise, you must be conscious of your weaknesses.

- Your educational background, past experience or even skills alone won't sell your "product". Your features and benefits, in the form of results that you have and will consistently attain, will.

- Keeping your current skills up to date, along with acquiring new ones that produce the results you sell, is the process you must become comfortable with if you are to be continuously investment-worthy and thus "employed".

• • • • •

You are what your deep, driving desire is.
As your desire is, so is your will.
As your will is, so is your deed.
As your deed is, so is your destiny.

—**BRIHADARANYAKA UPANISHAD IV. 4.5**

THREE

The Value Formula

Imagine that you are about to make a substantial purchase; say, a big-screen TV. It's expensive, and once you buy it you're going to have it around for years to come. What do you want to know before you're ready to shell out the cash? Likely you'll ask: Who made the TV I'm considering? Is that company an industry leader? Are the company and its products dependable? How long is the warranty? The list goes on and on.

We all understand that a product's value needs to be communicated in order for someone to buy it, but we're not used to thinking that way when it comes to our careers. We, after all, are people—not TV sets. What does buying a big-screen have to do with work security?

The answer is that to be a successful self-employed businessperson, you need to understand that you are your own "product." You must sell your product in much the same way dealers sell big-screen TVs—by persuasively communicating its value.

Look at it this way: the buyer is about to make a major purchase by buying the TV's enhanced entertainment capabilities. Before making that purchase, she wants to be certain that the TV will perform as advertised, that is, at a level that will create sufficient value for her and her family. It's the seller's job to convince the buyer that this is a good purchase.

Now translate that to the world of employment. The employer is about to make a major "purchase" by hiring your skills, knowledge, and/or labor. Before hiring you, the employer wants to be certain that you will perform as advertised, that is, to a level that will create sufficient value for the company. It's your job to convince the employer that "Hiring me is a good idea." The transaction has to be "worth it", whether you're selling that TV or applying for a new job.

You may, however, have trouble thinking of yourself as self-employed. You've grown up believing that security means depending on an employer to provide a paycheck: "If I am loyal, on time and at least reasonably hard-working, for a long enough period of time, my employer will reward me with a retirement package." It feels secure enough, so you follow the rules and try not to do anything that will jeopardize your "security".

You consider yourself "employed," not "self-employed". You don't see yourself as a product—perhaps partly because if you did, you might not want to buy what you're selling. Buyers want products with the highest possible value, not those offering less.

If you were your own product, wouldn't you want to have new features to promote to others—to explain why the new, improved You is much better than the old, unimproved You? To announce that this year's You has more value added, and thus is a bit more expensive than last year's You? And wouldn't you make sure that everyone involved in purchasing this year's You knew just how valuable you are (or can be) to the buyer? You would be your own sales brochure. You'd make sure that your buyers know that you have the biggest screen, the longest warranty, the clearest picture and sharpest sound—features unlike any other on the market, and at a price that's competitive. You would make sure: a) that your product was a superior value, and b) that people knew it!

Unfortunately, many people in today's workforce have lost awareness of their real value. Employees almost never consider themselves as products—or consider themselves from the employer's perspective. Applicants come to job interviews prepared simply to list their past accomplishments and their qualifications, just as you might read the specifications printed on the box that holds a new TV. With the TV, that tells you a lot about how the TV is likely to perform. But if you aren't aware of your own value, you cannot communicate it to others; and if you don't communicate your value, it's the same as if the TV salesperson simply said, "Here it is. Take it or leave it."

The applicant who does get the job believes she was hired because of her qualifications; if she doesn't, well, it was "out of my control." It's the same with layoffs: when was the last time you heard a recently "downsized" person say, "I got laid off because I wasn't adding enough value to the organization"? Probably never.

In truth, almost everything that has to do with your career is within your control. You can provide your own job security and, by doing so, never have to worry about your employment.

Here's the first step: if you want to gain control over your work security, you must begin by taking full responsibility for your career. You must think and act as though you are a successfully self-employed individual who has personally produced the results that have justified your paychecks.

You can't afford to allow your employer to provide for your working future. Even if today's employers wanted to offer you the same sort of security that your parents mistakenly thought they had, they could not. There are simply too many variables in our domestic and global economies for any single employer or industry to assure you of your livelihood. You can control your future only by creating it yourself.

Here are some empowering actions that you can take to achieve more career self-reliance and control over your working future.

Know Your Product's Values and Benefits

Whether you're applying for a job or undergoing an annual performance evaluation, the process is the same. Your objective during the course of the meeting is to clearly demonstrate to the interviewer or evaluator that your "product" (that is, yourself) will add or has added value to the organization well in excess of the product's cost. To do that successfully, you must be prepared to deal in specifics rather than generalities.

Before your meeting, make a list of your skills and strengths. Don't be modest, but at the same time don't stretch the truth. (Remember George O'Leary: Hired for his dream job as University of Notre Dame football coach, he lasted only five days when he was publicly fired for exaggerating his educational background on his résumé.) Identify the skills you have used and acquired both for pay and otherwise. Make the list as long as you can.

Next, organize the list. Place your five greatest skills or strengths at the top. Consider which of your strengths will be (or is) most valuable to this specific employer.

Then, for each skill or strength on the list, write a brief sentence or two clearly describing your actions that demonstrate your on-the-job use of that skill.

You are now ready to provide a list of your skills, along with specific ways that you have used these skills for your employer's benefit.

Finally, list the specific results you've achieved by applying your skills. These results must be in terms of dollars (saved or earned for the company), quantities, percentages and/or time. For many of us, this is the most challenging part of our preparation—too many of us are uncertain as to our specific value. But give this a try anyway—you may be pleasantly surprised at the results.

Preparing yourself to quantify your achievements, both verbally and with your written list, will separate you from the vast majority of other applicants and your coworkers. You will be able to talk and write about your features and benefits in terms of how much, how many, and how often—terms on which every employer has been forced to focus above all else. You will become your own "brochure", and potential/current employers will want the value you bring and will be willing to pay for it. And after all, the most valuable person in an organization usually doesn't have to fear being laid off. (But if you are laid off, the fact that you have a good sense of your own abilities and value will lessen the impact significantly. You'll know that there's another opportunity to contribute your value just down the street.)

Tooting Your Own Horn

As employees, when it comes to knowing and communicating your value you must learn to be far less modest than many of us are. Job interviews and performance evaluations are no place for subtlety.

Again, think about buying that big-screen TV. When you asked the salesperson about the set you were considering, did he hesitate, modestly, to list the set's advantages? Was he shy about telling you what it would do and how much you would enjoy owning it?

I would bet not. More likely, from the moment you entered the store you saw signs and banners with the manufacturer's name and logo calling out to you. Maybe you picked up a brochure or saw an ad on TV, on a billboard or in the newspaper, or maybe you even heard about the TV on the radio. None of this is subtle, and all of it is designed to make sure you know the product's value and to convince you that your life is just not complete without this specific TV.

Of course, the idea of walking into an interview or performance review with signs and banners is a little too Marx Brothers for the real world. But understanding that you are the one person who can best represent You is the crucial first step toward career success. Who, after all, knows you better than you? And if you don't toot your own horn, who will?

Whether it's an interview or an evaluation, be prepared to speak specifically about how your value relates to the job in question. Do some homework. Learn the "buyer's" particular needs. Check official job descriptions first, but don't be bashful about requesting any specific outcomes required from a particular position. In other words, find out exactly what the company expects and needs from this job, and communicate your value as it relates to those expectations and needs.

Preparing for an annual performance review is similar to preparing for an interview with a prospective employer. Both require you to be the best brochure-for-You that you can be. The big difference is that in preparing for a performance evaluation, it's essential that you know what results were expected during the period being reviewed.

Evaluations are designed to compare your specific achievements with the expected results. By knowing the expected results, you can prepare yourself to best communicate your value to the company.

In both interviews and evaluations, be prepared to identify and discuss your accomplishments and to offer detailed, written support for them. You'll want to keep an accurate diary of your accomplishments, updated at least monthly; this is a valuable source when you're creating your list of contributions. Presenting results-focused facts to interviewers and evaluators will help you assure a successful hiring or re-hiring.

You also must be scrupulously honest in describing your value to the company; there can be no bragging or boasting. Providing evidence of your contributions offers a clear record of your accomplishments, which should be offered with enthusiasm and conviction. This kind of presentation, whether an interview or evaluation, tells the listener that you are a "doer" and that you represent yourself with facts, not mere speculation, about your performance.

Your Value Formula

The concept of "value" is familiar to you. As a consumer, you seek value in everything you purchase. Yet when it comes to determining your own specific value, you may not know where to begin. Even if you feel valuable, you may be hard-pressed to state specifically how and why your employers should prize you. You may be more comfortable explaining the value of that TV set than yourself. Strange, but true.

Here's a formula that will help you overcome that oddity forever:

The "Value of You" Formula:

$$V = St + A + R$$

or

Value = Strengths + Actions + Results

This formula can help you assess your own value. By using the Value Formula, you can clearly see your specific value and, just as importantly, you can easily identify areas where you need to add more value by improving yourself. Let's take a closer look at each part of the formula.

Strengths

Strengths and skills are the things at which you excel—the areas in which you perform at or above your employer's expectations. Some of these may result from formal education; others may be inherent in our personalities, such as being a good listener. Still others may have resulted from our ongoing experience; and some strengths come from a combination of education, personality traits and experience.

Don't be too sure that you already know all of your strengths. Most people don't. In fact, many people are pleasantly surprised once they take the time to write down their strengths and skills. Consider dividing your own list by category. Begin with your formal education, including not only high school and college, but also any seminars or training where you learned something that's valuable to you on the job.

Don't forget to include strengths and skills acquired on the job. Perhaps you were part of a team that launched a new product or handled the changeover to a new accounting or computer system. Maybe you helped with a major restructuring of the company, or with the transition when your company was acquired by a larger firm. All of these on-the-job experiences, assuming you learned from them, can increase the value of You.

Listing your formal education, by the way, doesn't mean merely writing down the year you graduated. For instance: Were your math grades excellent? That's one of your strengths. Your degree may not be in accounting, but being good with numbers is a strength that adds to your total value.

Next, consider your inner self—your personality traits. Have you always been told that you're easy to talk to, or energetic, or detail-oriented? Does leading groups come easily to you? Are you at home in competitive situations? Are you a team player? All of these traits, though not necessarily the result of formal training, can be important to your employer in assessing your value.

Review your list with colleagues, friends and family. You'll be pleasantly surprised at the strengths they see in you that you haven't identified. Add their suggestions to your list.

Actions

If Strengths are the things you can do, then Actions are the things you do that demonstrate or apply your strengths. From creating a new filing system, to leading a total quality initiative, to organizing a company baseball team, your actions are tangible proof of how you have applied your strengths and skills. Don't expect your employer to know—or remember—your past actions; it's your responsibility to identify and communicate the successes that have resulted from you applying your skills.

Results

Results are the bottom line of every business venture. You may have terrific strengths, and you may have applied those strengths, but without positive results there's no real value being created. Here's an example:

Let's say that in school you did very well in a project management class; that's one of your strengths. Your personality is detail-oriented and you've always considered yourself a leader; that's also listed among your strengths. With these strengths in your arsenal, you decide to organize a company picnic and softball game and the day goes off without a hitch—it's a big success.

But what results were created? Sure, you used your leadership skills and took action. You worked hard and everyone enjoyed the day, but was any real value created? The answer is absolutely "yes," but it's your responsibility to identify and document the specific results and then be able to communicate them in terms of value to the company.

The results of your actions in this example can take many forms.

- Your skills in organizing and delegating resulted in an efficient planning process, which allowed the event to be less costly than in past years.

- Your leadership skills in planning and carrying out the day contributed to improving your coworkers' morale, which reduced turnover.

- The event itself generated conversations between workers in departments that don't necessarily communicate with each other, which improved efficiency and reduced overhead costs.

- An atmosphere of teamwork and "we're all in this together" permeated the day and spilled over into the workplace. (Perhaps grouchy old security guy Stan was seen to laugh out loud, something no one in the company remembers ever happening before.)

To support these claimed results, you need a record of the dollars saved (over last year's picnic, for instance) or some evidence of the improved morale and its resulting positive impact (maybe you have a photo of stunned coworkers staring at a laughing Stan).

$$So: V = St + A + R$$

It's up to you to record and document your results in dollars, numbers, percentages or time. Then, using the formula as your outline, you can communicate the quantified value of You.

In shopping for real estate, it's said the three most important things to look for are "location, location and location." When you're securing your working future, the three most important things are value, value and value. Identifying your contributions and being adept at effectively communicating them will separate you from the competition and also provide motivation for you to continue to add and build strengths; to take new actions; and to stockpile positive results, all of which only increase your value.

It's unfortunate that in today's workplace few people truly understand their own value. This understanding helps you look for ways to increase your value by finding opportunities to solve problems, apply creativity, collaborate with coworkers and contribute greater results overall.

Without a clear picture of your value, you cannot begin to see what you might improve. And just as with any product, if you don't improve and move forward, you fall behind. It's your value that will show your current or next employer that you are an investment that has produced, and will continue to produce, a solid return.

CASE STUDY: FRAN'S STORY

Removing the Blinders

Fran was a production worker at Acme Mfg., a large company that made women's clothing. She'd worked for Acme for almost thirty years, and Acme was the only employer she'd ever had. Fran was the most loyal of employees, was always on time, and had a near-perfect attendance record—so you can imagine her shock when Acme announced a massive layoff and told Fran she was among those to go.

Like her laid-off coworkers, especially those with long tenure, Fran was devastated. She felt cheated. It wasn't fair. Why would the company—the one to which she'd been so faithful—do this to her?

Of course, Acme didn't actually think it was doing something to Fran. It had been under increasing pressure from overseas competitors to reduce costs. The company held on as long as it could, but finally decided to close its U.S. plant and make its garments where labor costs were lower. Acme saw only two choices: close Fran's plant or go out of business altogether.

"Nervous" doesn't even begin to describe Fran's feelings about finding another job. She thought she had little value outside of Acme. She knew the job market was highly competitive, and felt that at her age there was little hope of being hired again, that she'd never be able to interest another employer.

Fran was convinced that Acme had been the source of her employment security. She had no idea what her real value was, or why anyone would want to hire her. She couldn't, however, have been more wrong about herself and her marketability.

In fact, Fran had been promoted seventeen times in her thirty years with Acme. She had successfully interviewed and competed for each new position, and her compensation had steadily increased as her job increased in complexity, responsibility and importance. Her assignments had taken her all over the plant, top to bottom, end to end. Along the way she had acquired many valuable production, communication and collaboration skills. She had progressed from working alone to being responsible for the output of groups of workers, and had volunteered on several task forces that had met plant-wide needs such as process improvements, teamwork and quality control. In addition, she received a great deal of training as new equipment and procedures had been installed. She even taught some of the training programs herself.

It was only when she was challenged about her perceived lack of value that Fran, reluctantly at first, came to understand that she had *earned* each of her new positions by consistently producing the results required. She had brought value to Acme and it had really been she, not her employer, who had been responsible for her employment security all along.

These insights made a world of difference to Fran. She had seen herself as just another out-of-work senior employee, lost in the shuffle in a viciously competitive job market. She now knew that she had been a valuable contributor to an increasingly complex production process, both on her own and by passing her knowledge along to others. She realized that she had many years of demonstrated initiative, skills and results that would make her a strong candidate for any position she wanted on the open market, just as she had been during her years at Acme.

As it turned out, Fran actually hadn't been "fired" at all. She had been "freed", not only to appreciate her own many contributions to Acme's success, but to realize a return on *Acme's investment in her* by getting an even better position elsewhere.

Know Yourself—Know Your Value

There is no question that in successfully charting the course of your career, knowing and being able to communicate your value is of paramount importance. By itself, knowing and communicating your value may be enough to create success in your career, but there's another very important issue to consider before embarking on your journey.

That issue is *you*. Who are you? What do you enjoy doing? What don't you enjoy? You need to know something about yourself—your inner tendencies, your preferences. Being self-aware is priceless when making career choices, with respect to where you want to work and how you relate to fellow employees.

Simply put, if you know what you like, perhaps you can find work doing that (or doing something similar or in a related field). If you don't know what you *do* like, do you know what you *don't* like? With that knowledge, at least you can steer clear of options that truly don't suit you.

The bottom line is that if you like what you do, you'll do far better at it (and in your life) than if you're doing something you don't like doing.

The first step in identifying what you like to do is a self-evaluation. Ask yourself questions:

- Do I prefer a desk job or being outside the office?
- Do I like being in the limelight, or am I happier behind the scenes?
- Am I a better listener or talker?
- Do I enjoy using my creativity on the job, or do I prefer more structure?
- Do I enjoy working with a team or do I prefer working alone?
- Am I a problem solver, or do I hate identifying and solving new challenges?
- Do I want to travel on business or stay at home?
- Do I want to work a set schedule or a varied one?

The answers to these questions and others will help you avoid opportunities that don't mesh with your personal wants and needs. You'll pursue the possibilities that have at least some features you enjoy, and as a result you're more likely to find greater career success because you like what you're doing and how you're doing it.

While you're conducting this self-examination, it may help to consider that there are generally four main categories of people-types: Humanists, Energizers, Organizers and Futurists.

- Humanists are concerned with unity and harmony, and with the feelings of the people involved in any venture.
- Energizers are open to the possibilities for productive change, and are active in starting and implementing change.
- Organizers prefer structure.
- Futurists are most interested in knowledge and thinking.

We all know people who fit into each of these categories. In which of these four would you place yourself?

Certainly, we all have elements of each of these four types, and there is considerable overlap in every human being. But usually one category will apply a little more than the others. The degree to which you prefer one over another can dramatically influence your career choices and, ultimately, your life.

Humanists, for instance, are often found in the clergy, as social workers and in personnel or human resources departments. Energizers are happiest in careers involving sales, entertainment and athletics, among others. Organizers make excellent doctors, lawyers and accountants, all of whom do things "by the numbers." Many Futurists end up as writers, teachers and scientists.

Business organizations are made up of people who fall into each of these four categories, which is absolutely necessary if an organization is to remain vibrant and alive. A business full of Futurists, for example, would not survive long in a fast-paced, highly competitive industry. However, a company would do very well if it hired Futurists and Organizers to think through and generate long-term strategic planning and product development, and employed Humanists to manage customer relations.

It's often very easy to tell when someone is working in a career that's not in sync with his tendencies; we've all encountered them. Imagine an Organizer as a rock-concert promoter, where no two projects are alike. And an Energizer would lose her mind in the rigid, structured world of, say, insurance. It's not a pretty picture.

Knowing which categories apply to your bosses or peers is also helpful in developing effective communication and good working relationships with them. Your presentation to an Organizer is much different than the one you would give to an Energizer. The Organizer needs detailed information, all the t's crossed and the i's dotted. The Energizer would lose interest in that much detail; better you should be fast, providing only the vital information needed to make a good, quick decision.

The real challenge is in working with groups of people, which usually includes a mix of preferences, tendencies and categories. Diversity is best managed when it's understood. Knowing your own general category and appreciating your coworkers' types is key. Together, they form the foundation of great individual and team-work. Better knowledge of yourself and others can make you more productive, thus increasing your value as well as your satisfaction.

Setting Goals

Let's suppose that you now know your "product", (You) and you've identified your strengths, recorded your actions and documented your results. You're ready to go out into the world and present the new, more valuable You. Whether you're seeking a promotion, a change within your current company or a job with a new employer, having well thought-out goals for your "product" and its further development is important in controlling your career.

Setting career goals means making difficult choices, and it involves deciding what matters most to you. Goal-setting requires knowing that your needs and priorities may change—and if they do, you may need to change your goals. Goal-setting is not a one-time action, but a process that evolves and lasts over a lifetime.

Identify what's most important to you. Is it the industry, the work, the pay or the benefits? Is it important where you work (geographically as well as within the building)? How about your office size, your title, the working conditions, your reporting hierarchy, your associates, the commuting distance, the size of the company and/or your opportunities for advancement and growth?

Knowing and ranking these elements—along with others that are significant to you, such as athletics, hobbies or family—will help you lift any fog and clearly see the path before you.

Lights! Camera! Action! Preparing Your Own Business Plan

Once your goals have been established, it's necessary to develop a plan to ensure you meet those objectives. The plan should list any specific actions you must take in order to achieve your goals within your desired time frame.

- Will you need any additional education or training? If so, where, when and at what cost?
- Is additional work experience required? If so, what kind, and what are your steps to acquiring it?
- What resources, if any, do you need to accomplish your goals?

These are the questions you must ask and answer in order to develop an action plan for achieving your goals. It's hard work, but it's a process you must undertake to successfully sell your "product" to the "buyer" you most want to attract.

Employee/Employer "Wish" Lists

*What **you** want more of from your employer:*

1. Satisfaction
2. Recognition
3. Control/Security
4. Opportunities
5. Rewards

*What your **employer** wants more of from you:*

1. Results
2. Commitment
3. Self-direction
4. Creativity
5. Value

Critical Employability Strengths

- **Attitude**—You must have a positive outlook in order to market yourself effectively.

- **Assessing**—Your marketable strengths must be identified.

- **Communicating**—You must be prepared to communicate your strengths, both verbally and in writing.

- **Quantifying**—You must be able to quantify the results you have achieved from applying your strengths.

- **Planning**—You must plan the steps required for you to achieve your career goals.

- **Résumé Writing**—You must write an effective, results-focused, self-marketing "brochure" or record of accomplishments.

- **Interviewing**—You must be able to demonstrate—clearly and specifically—how your strengths match the requirements of the position you're seeking.

- **Goal-setting**—You must establish reasonable goals for yourself that are consistent with your strengths and career interests.

- **Researching**—You must be aware of the resources available to help you identify your targeted work.

- **Decision-making**—You must have the ability to select from among the various career and work opportunities that are available to you.

- **Measuring Performance**—You must be able to measure your own performance and match it against your action plan.

- **Networking**—You must have the ability to remain connected with past and present associates and friends so you can help each other meet your career goals.

- **Negotiating**—You must be sufficiently focused on your ability to contribute so that you can persuade employers to meet your economic and other career needs.

- **Preparation**—You must control your career by taking full advantage of all available learning opportunities that are consistent with your career goals.

REMEMBER YOUR...

STRENGTHS + ACTIONS + RESULTS

= YOUR VALUE

Some pursue happiness, others create it.

—ANONYMOUS

Chapter 3: Checkpoints for Learning

Some basic principles for achieving more career self-reliance and control over your working future include the following:

- To be a successful self-employed businessperson, you need to understand that you are your own "product".

- You need to know your product's unique features and benefits—your skills, strengths, achievements, qualities and attributes.

- You need to toot your own horn at job interviews and performance evaluations—present the facts about your performance and let them speak to your value.

- The Value Formula: Strengths + Actions + Results = Your Value

- Your strengths and skills are the things at which you excel.

- Your actions are the things that you do which demonstrate or apply your strengths.

- Results are the bottom line of every business venture, including yours.

- If you like what you do, you will be much better at it than if you don't like what you do.

- Know which category best describes yourself and your coworkers:
  - Humanist
  - Organizer

    - Energizer
    - Futurist

- Well thought-out goals and an action/business plan to meet your goals are important steps in controlling your career.

● ● ● ● ●

That's what real learning is—
seeing something you've always known,
but in a different way.

—Doris Lessing

FOUR

Déjà Vu

Please go back and re-read Chapter 3: The Value Formula. As with the second (or third or fourteenth) time through a Mark Twain novel, Mozart's "The Magic Flute", or a favorite movie, you're likely to notice something of value that you hadn't fully appreciated the first time.

• • • • •

From the boardroom to the factory floor, work is understood more and more clearly as an expression of thought.

—NATHANIEL BRANDON

FIVE

Kaizen: Continuously Building Your Value for Long-Term Success

It's no secret that, among the long list of countries that now successfully compete with the United States, Japan's example of commitment to continuous quality offers much that we can and must learn. Business schools across the United States, and countless books and seminars, dissect and analyze how Japan created and maintains its standard of excellence in manufacturing. Remember, it wasn't long ago that "Made in Japan" meant "cheap"; today, it means "of the highest quality."

Of all the business-related concepts Japan has utilized, none has received as much attention on our side of the Pacific as "Kaizen." And Kaizen is as essential to you as realizing that you are a valuable product; it's as important as anything you've learned thus far. Here's why.

Kaizen can best be defined as "continuous quality improvement." It means that even though this year's You is pretty terrific, if next year's version isn't somehow better, your value doesn't increase and you risk falling behind your coworker-competitors. American companies learned, too often the hard way, that without a concentrated effort to continuously improve their products, consumers would stop buying them in favor of a higher quality, even though foreign-made, alternative. The days of American consumers being willing to purchase whatever U.S. corporations produce simply because the product is American-made are long past. Do you?

But the product we're talking about here is You, and how your value as a product is the only true source of work security and financial success. So how does Kaizen affect You? You simply cannot afford to stand still. Even if you're this year's Employee of the Year, what about next year? To avoid being like the many American companies that have learned the hard way, you must make a constant and focused effort to continuously improve your own product: You.

There are many ways to build Kaizen into your self-product. (See the list at the end of this Chapter.) Two of the easiest and most obvious ways, though, are education and volunteering.

Learn to Want to Learn

It's heartening to see that more and more adults are returning to school every year. The future is all about our skills and the proven ability to apply them to produce quantifiable results. And although volunteering has much to offer in terms of personal satisfaction as well as career benefit (see the following section), there is no substitute for formal education when you're honing and adding to your skills and strengths. Too many of us, however, see continuing education as something to avoid.

Why do so many of us seem to resist learning? Is it the thought of sitting in a classroom? Or the memory of a teacher who was known (for good reason) as The Hatchet? Just the idea of having to study gives many of us cold chills. Some say it's the fault of our public schools; others explain it in terms of the human condition. Regardless, the aversion to learning is easily changed, especially for adults.

CASE STUDY: JILL'S STORY

Better Late Than Never

Jill was a mediocre student in high school, and graduated knowing only one thing for sure: classrooms were not the place for her. She went to work instead of college, and it wasn't until almost 25 years later that she decided to take one class at a local community college, just to see if anything had changed.

She found college to be an entirely different place than her high-school years led her to expect. To her amazement, she found that her life and work experience—and her lifelong love of reading—had given her a strong foundation for college. The way she described it, "I found that just living my life had taught me a tremendous amount. It had given me many more mental 'hooks' that easily latched onto the classroom material."

After that first community-college class, Jill became a full-time student. Two years later she transferred to a university, and two years after that she received not only her Bachelor's degree but also invitations to graduate school from several colleges nationwide. Through her college classes, though, Jill realized that her dream had always been to write. So she hung out her shingle as a freelance writer-for-hire, and today she works on everything from business and promotional materials, to family histories, to scientific and technical reports. She's not financially rich, but every day she wakes up knowing she's doing something she loves.

Not everyone will, can or wants to do what Jill did. (For instance, as a full-time student Jill also held two part-time jobs in order to pay for her schooling.) But she found that as an adult student, with real-life experiences and knowledge behind her, learning became a pleasure. It was energizing, absorbing and even addictive: once you start learning, you want to learn more.

One of Jill's biggest fears about starting college had been that her age would make her an outsider, shunned by her much-younger student colleagues. She was so uncertain about this that for the first month of her community college classes she ate lunch in her car, alone, convinced that no one on campus would want to eat and talk with her. But soon she found that the information was the great leveler: If several people in Calculus class were struggling with a rate-of-change assignment, for instance, they worked together. It didn't matter that the chronological ages might range from Sammy's 19 to Jill's 40; what mattered was that they all wanted to understand the material.

If you really want security in today's world, it's important for you to develop or increase your desire to learn. The more you know and the more skills you possess, the more control you'll have over your career and the more work/financial security you'll enjoy.

Computer technology is making it both easier and more convenient for you to expand your knowledge. Colleges, universities and trade schools are making themselves readily available through your personal computer. Soon, technology will allow you to have live, fully interactive, on-demand classrooms at work and at home through your computer and TV.

These same colleges, universities and trade schools are also making themselves more accessible to people who work full-time; offering evening and weekend extension courses designed specifically for people who have jobs and families to consider.

Another advantage is that college courses may lead you in directions you hadn't expected—you may discover you have a gift for archeology or art history or public speaking that you'll want to pursue as a career. Even if you don't change career directions, your professor(s), who are generally very encouraging to and supportive of adult students, may be valuable sources of information, suggestions and references.

This widespread availability of continuing education, while providing learning opportunities for more and more people, will ultimately make workplace competition even more intense. If you're not taking advantage of the chance to increase your knowledge, you can bet that your coworker is. And because this education is so widely available, your not taking advantage of it will send a clear signal that you are not interested in improving your skills or increasing your value and thus your competitiveness.

On the other hand, by learning to enjoy learning, and then adding to your skills (and results) list every year, you will continually be increasing your value to your company and gaining more and more control over your own career and work stability.

Learning Opportunities

While you are with any employer, take advantage of all seminars and workshops the company offers. Consider devoting a set amount of your monthly earnings to continuing education. Many employers offer tuition assistance programs for employees who are taking courses related to their industry or who are pursuing a degree. Check into these—the more support your employer will give, the better.

If you're between jobs, learning is even more important. The extra time you have while unemployed is ideal for catching up on business/industry developments. (This doesn't have to be in a classroom. Pick up journals and magazines published by and for your industry, and read one every day.)

Many business-related seminars are offered at no charge. Take full advantage of the ones that relate to your career objectives. Talk to your local community college or university about being allowed to audit courses—that is, to sit in on the class without receiving a grade or taking tests—often at little or no charge. Classes may take place in the evenings or on weekends, but if bending your schedule a bit means getting free or low-cost knowledge that can be turned into marketable skills, there's no question: *do it.*

Like employment, success and goal-setting, education is clearly a process rather than an event. Knowledge, like gold, is where you find it. The continued search for and acquiring of new skills that can help you to produce more and better results will contribute to your employment security and increase the market value of your continuously improving product: *yourself.*

Again, Why Do I Need to Keep Learning?

It's the 21st century. These days, successful business owners are thinking in terms of dollars and "sense". They understand that they need to make a certain profit, say, 25 percent, on each employee over and above the employee's cost to the company. It's just good management: every employee must contribute to the company more than s/he costs or the company cannot continue to operate.

By understanding this fundamental business principle, you gain a clear advantage when applying for a job. You affirm to your prospective employer that you believe in your ability to add value; that you're not remaining stationary, but you're continuing to learn and to keep up with your industry; and that you will negotiate a compensation package that's based on results.

When you exceed the desired performance (as I know you will), you're on solid ground in asking for an increase in compensation. On the other hand, if the agreed-to results are not delivered, then you can expect a performance re-evaluation or even a reduction in compensation.

But what if returning to school isn't something you're ready to do? What can you do outside of your workplace that can have a tangible effect on your value and your career?

You Can Volunteer

Volunteering is an excellent and all too often over-looked way to develop new skills and relationships while contributing much-needed help to worthwhile organizations such as your church, community groups, the local PTA and countless others—and these new skills and the results they produce will only increase your value, to yourself and your community as well as your employer.

Likewise, the relationships you develop while volunteering become part of your network of supporters as you begin actively marketing yourself. Think about this: It was Bill Gates' mother who introduced Gates, now the world's richest man, to the Chief Executive Officer of IBM. Mom Gates knew the CEO because they were both volunteer members of a Red Cross board. Perhaps Bill Gates would have met the CEO anyway; perhaps not. But just think of the immediate rapport you have with the person you meet when you're both working for the benefit of some other person or group.

Before You Sign Up

Before you begin volunteering, there are several important guidelines you need to consider.

First, take your volunteer work seriously—at least as seriously as you take your on-the-job responsibilities, if not more so. The fact that you're not being paid is no excuse for slacking off, missing deadlines, or not doing what you said you'd do. If you just want the name

("I'm a Special Olympics volunteer") without playing the game (actually showing up to help with events), then volunteering probably isn't for you. In fact, if you're going to gain from the volunteer experience and benefit from the time you're investing, you'll want to perform well beyond expectations or promises.

Second, be careful not to spread yourself too thin. Don't let quantity become more important than quality. Be selective. Volunteer your time only to those organizations whose missions are important to you. Remember: There will be hard work involved, so it's best if you're working toward something you already care about. Look for groups, events and activities that hold your interest. Are you concerned with the public school system, people living with illness or infirmity, homeless people, or kids who need an adult mentor? Then you'll want to look into classroom aide programs, Meals on Wheels, a local homeless shelter or soup kitchen, or Big Brothers/Big Sisters. The opportunities and the need for volunteers are endless, and only you can decide what to include on your list.

Third, find a volunteer opportunity that relates to your work. If you want to go into nursing, for instance, stop by your local hospital and ask about their volunteer programs (every hospital has them), or call the local Red Cross chapter. If your goal is to become a teacher, talk to local schools about volunteering as a classroom or playground aide, or maybe a tutor. Are you a carpenter or potential carpenter? Call Habitat for Humanity, or maybe a local church group that helps elderly and infirm people, or those who don't have the money, to maintain their homes.

Fourth, enjoy yourself. Some people insist that there's no such thing as a truly selfless act—that everything we do for others provides some benefit to ourselves—and maybe that's so. But the sheer pleasure of being part of a group that's giving people something they might not be able to obtain otherwise—whether it's repaired front steps, or a ride to the doctor's office, or a hot meal, or help with algebra—is indescribable. Aside from what you'll gain in terms of networking, experience, etc., when you volunteer you're going to feel like one of the planet's Good Guys, and that feeling has value too.

The Benefits of Volunteering

As mentioned, volunteering for any worthy organization is fulfilling. But in addition to that, when you align your volunteer time and effort with your career objectives, you reap even greater rewards—and during the times, which always seem to happen now and then, that your volunteer responsibilities become larger than you had planned, you'll find motivation in the fact that your volunteer work rests on a foundation of your life interests and career goals. When the time comes for references, recommendations or contacts, this type of recognized outstanding service can be just like money in the bank.

Another of the many benefits of volunteering comes from interacting with and learning from your fellow volunteers who, like you, are doing this because they choose to, not because they have to. Volunteer work is unlike any conventional job atmosphere or culture. It requires skills that, when transferred to your "paid" job, greatly enhance your total value.

Getting things accomplished in a volunteer setting is not about imposing organizational authority. It's about collaboration, perhaps even synergy; getting people to "buy in" and want to work hard for the personal satisfaction of accomplishing something for the common good. Volunteer work involves persuasion, not simply an authoritarian "do this because I said to."

As a volunteer, you develop your persuasive skills as a matter of necessity. These are some of the most important skills you can possess: they allow you to become more effective at communicating and gaining support for your initiatives. People who are good persuaders will never have to worry about their employability in any business environment.

Volunteering, if done right, benefits everyone: you, the organization and people that receive your volunteer services, your fellow volunteers, the community at large—you all win. It can be hard work—from the service itself to organizing your own schedule to fit it in—but it can benefit your career while, even more importantly, adding a richness and an even greater sense of purpose to your life.

A Final Word

The key to a mutually profitable results/reward relationship is open communication about "what's expected and why" between you and your employer. Producing the required results obviously benefits the employer, but it's also good for you. Such results build your inventory of accomplishments. That inventory provides employment security with the current employer. Similarly, since your accomplishments, like your skills, are portable, it also adds to your employability and value elsewhere.

Japanese companies have long since recognized the critical importance of continuous product improvement, or Kaizen. That very thinking has led Japanese companies to produce products that are among the most sought-after goods the world has to offer—products that consistently meet or exceed expectations, products that produce the results sought by their buyers.

In today's workplace you are the product and, like any product, you must continuously strive to improve yourself and increase your market value. Through education and volunteering, your product will continue to increase in value and your source of work security will have been enhanced forever. And even better, *the improvement will have come from inside, not outside.*

Seven Keys to Building Your Kaizen

I. Entrepreneuring
- Identify your unique "product"/"business"
- Establish clear "business" goals
- Produce specific results

II. Self-Relying
- No codependence
- Be independent and interdependent
- Be self-employed

III. Marketing/Networking
- Know your customer(s)
- Build strategic alliances
- Be visible

IV. Learning
- Continuous process, not an event
- Self-directed/assessed
- "Product" research and development

V. Diversifying
- Build/acquire new marketable skills
- Find new opportunities
- "Moonlight" at something that interests you—a secret passion

VI. Challenge-Seeking
- Find growth opportunities
- Avoid the "comfort zone"
- Take informed risks

VII. Balancing
- Personal and professional commitments
- Relaxing/producing
- Be self-disciplined: mind/body/work

• • • • •

Chapter 5: Checkpoints for Learning

- The Japanese business-related concept Kaizen is defined as "continuous quality improvement," which can be applied to your own product: You.

- Some keys to continuous quality improvement include:
    - Learning to want to learn
    - Volunteering

- Volunteering can result in building your inventory of accomplishments that can enhance your current work security and future employability.

- In today's workplace You are the product, and like any product you must continuously strive to improve yourself—as you do through volunteering and continuing education.

- Quality, like value, requires personal commitment and, thus, is an "inside job."

• • • • •

Knowledge and competence are replacing rank as the voice of authority.

–**Nathaniel Brandon**

SIX

Personal Mastery: Controlling Your Own Future

For many years, people have wondered what makes humans behave as we do. The human species has always been an intriguing subject of study, and answers are difficult to come by. Typical questions are: Why do we do what we do? What makes some people happier than others? How can two people go through the same experience and interpret it in totally different ways?

Even more so today, when life is full of modern conveniences and we seem to have more choices about how to spend our time, people find themselves wondering: What is happiness for me? How can success, satisfaction and joy be achieved by me? This chapter focuses on the idea of personal mastery, which encompasses what you might say is "the road to getting what you want out of life."

What Is Personal Mastery?

"Personal" correctly implies that the process involves one person and is different for everyone. This is not something that's done as a group or is done to you by someone else (the way the hygienist cleans your teeth). Instead, we "do it" to/for ourselves, by ourselves. "Mastery" means having proficient skills in an area, or "the capacity not only to produce results, but also to 'master' the principles underlying the way you produce results." Putting the two words together gives the impression of producing results and having skills with regard to one's own being. Mastering your "self" involves developing your ability to decide what you want, and putting into practice the activities necessary for you to achieve your goals.

Personal mastery means continually expanding yourself and your abilities to achieve the results you desire in life. There are two basic concepts to understand in relation to personal mastery: vision and understanding.

First, you have to have a vision or desired state. This can take a wide variety of appearances but, in essence, it is something important to you that you are willing to work for. Your personal vision provides purpose, direction and focus. It allows you to get where you want to go. You create a personal vision/mission in order to feel successful, happy and satisfied.

The second aspect, which may be less obvious, involves having a clear understanding of current reality. It's critical that you know where you are so you can identify the necessary steps to reaching your vision. (Imagine yourself keeping an appointment in a strange town. Even with a detailed map in hand, if you don't know where you are, you won't have a clue about how to get where you're going.) If you have an unrealistic picture of where you are today, any "map" of how to get from Here to There will be skewed.

Personal mastery, then, is a process of getting from where you are to where you want to be, while being honest with yourself about exactly where those places are.

The discrepancy between Where You Are and Where You Want To Be is referred to as "creative tension". Different from the normal definition of the word "tension", creative tension is something to excite and energize you, a challenge. Although you constantly strive to reduce the creative tension, you also strive to create more of it by expanding your vision. By creating this tension within yourself, you can more easily pull yourself toward your goals. Not by eliminating the tension, but by balancing and shaping it, can you achieve what you really desire.

It is only by setting challenging goals for yourself that you can expect to have the drive and ambition to move forward in your life. As you develop personal mastery, you will gain a better understanding for where the balance lies. The tension needs to be strong enough to cause you to act, yet not so strong that you lose hope and give up.

People who have attained personal mastery follow a common path to success:

- First, they know their outcomes; that is, specifically and precisely, they define what they want.
- Second, they take action.

- Third, they recognize the kinds of responses and results they're getting from their actions, and note as quickly as possible if those steps are bringing them closer to or farther from their goals.
- Fourth, they develop the flexibility to modify their behavior until they get what they're aiming for.

The general idea is that you can get whatever you want; you just have to be able to identify what it is. Being able to stand out from the rest and make an impact requires you to be committed; to believe in the possibility that you can obtain anything you truly want; to organize and use your resources; to clarify your values; to focus your energy; to effectively communicate and bond with others; and, above all, to be honest with yourself while engaging in all of the above. Developing these qualities within yourself takes a lifetime of work. But doing so gives you the power both to see clearly what you want and to take the actions necessary to achieve it.

What Are The Characteristics of People with High Levels of Personal Mastery?

1. They have a special sense of purpose that lies behind their visions and goals.
2. They see current reality as an ally, not an enemy.
3. They welcome change, rather than resist it.
4. They have an inquisitive attitude about reality.
5. They have a feeling of connection to others and to life.
6. They feel they have influence, but not total control, over their environment.

7. They have a feeling of movement, but never arrival. (The journey is the reward.)

8. They have confidence, along with a strong awareness of their own limitations.

These qualities can be applied narrowly to individuals, as well as broadly to systems and organizations. The underlying theme involves taking a proactive, purposeful approach to attaining the goals and results you desire. Whether it's a person, a family or a billion-dollar company, when there is a *will* to accomplish something and an understanding about *how* to achieve it, success is a likely outcome.

How Is Personal Mastery Different from Other Concepts?

Over the years, many concepts have been studied and defined that resemble personal mastery or some aspect of it. As researchers have wondered what makes people do what they do, various models and theories have emerged. It is important to keep in mind, though, that the words used are much less important than the changes in thought and action that accompany the development of personal mastery.

Here's how personal mastery compares with some of these other concepts:

Agency. Agency can be defined as human motivation for individual differentiation, involving a striving for mastery, self-discipline and achievement. Although agency may encompass some aspects of personal mastery, it also includes striving for superiority, competition, autonomy and the need for the power to make the right choices.

Coping. Coping is a way for people to deal with everyday strains and stresses. The main difference between coping and personal mastery is that coping focuses on minimizing the discomforts of life, but coping is not directed at the root causes of problems or at fundamental change. Coping treats symptoms, not causes. The main ways that people cope are:

1. Trying to alter the situation ("I'm going to change whatever I can to make this better.")

2. Trying to change their perception of the situation by denying that which is uncomfortable ("I'll just pretend this isn't happening.")

3. Managing the stress by accommodating to it without being overwhelmed ("This, too, shall pass.")

These actions are very common in everyday activities, and it's important that you not mistake them for working toward personal mastery.

Self-Efficacy. The definition of "efficacy" is "the power to produce an effect." Self-efficacy centers on the expectations people have for their own success. People set standards against which they evaluate their performance, and they create inducements to help them persist until their performance matches their standards. It may be important to have high self-efficacy to move toward personal mastery, but personal mastery requires more thought and definition about what is desired.

Motivation. Motivation is generally thought of as a person's reasons for doing something. Motivation involves a willingness to take risks, overcome obstacles, explore options and assume responsibility for making a decision. Personal mastery, however, delves deeper into a person's specific goals and desires, and it provides a framework to use in reaching these goals.

Hardiness. Hardiness typically refers to a person's physical health and stamina, and is defined as "a personality construct or characteristic that enables people to remain healthy and adapt to various illnesses." In comparison to personal mastery, hardiness describes what you are moving away from more than what you are moving toward.

Self-Actualization. Noted psychologist Abraham H. Maslow (1908–1970) is credited with developing the term "self-actualization", which describes a holistic approach to life, defining how a happy, healthy, well-functioning person behaves. When a person's physiological, safety, belonging and esteem needs have been met, the self-actualized personality emerges. We may see personal mastery as advancing the idea of self-actualization, offering more concrete avenues to help people reach their potential.

Personal mastery goes beyond these typical concepts because it gives you guidance on how to achieve your desired state. Although there are overlaps with these other concepts, personal mastery gets at the heart of the matter. It forces you to "take ownership" of your own destiny, and thus it supports a permanent change in the way you see yourself.

These other concepts, especially self-actualization and motivation, are also important and deserve some attention. The ideas behind self-actualization are very similar to those of personal mastery, and motivation is an important element in moving you toward your goals. Personal mastery takes the best of these concepts and combines them to help you establish a process within yourself to enable you to accomplish your vision.

One advantage of personal mastery is that once the techniques and ideas are learned, the process feeds on itself. It is not a constant battle to force yourself to take steps toward your vision—instead, you realize that you have the power to do and undo anything that comes between you what you want to happen. This insight, ultimately, makes personal mastery the "straight line" that best connects where you are with where you want to be.

The skill to do comes of doing.

—R. W. EMERSON

Chapter 6: Checkpoints for Learning

- Personal mastery means continually expanding yourself and your abilities to achieve the results you want in your life.

- "Creative tension" is the gap between where you are and where you want to be. That "tension" needs to be strong enough to cause you to act, yet not so strong that you see no hope of achieving your goals and give up.

- People who have achieved personal mastery:
  - find purpose in their lives
  - welcome change
  - are inquisitive
  - feel connected to themselves as well as others
  - see life as a challenging journey, and, most importantly, *choose to be proactive participants in that journey.*

- Personal mastery starts with seeing yourself as an individual who is able to cope with life's challenges—but even more, it means taking full responsibility for creating your personal vision and then *making it happen.*

• • • • •

The world is moved not only by the mighty shoves of heroes, but also by the aggregate of the tiny pushes of each honest worker.

—HELEN KELLER

SEVEN

Family *Matters*

Your family's love and support is an asset that cannot be overstated or sufficiently appreciated. As it relates to the workplace, family support that comes from people who understand your perspective on your career, who recognize your goals and who believe in what you are trying to accomplish, is invaluable. Conversely, however, family support that lacks this understanding can, with the best of intentions, hold you back or otherwise alter your intended direction.

(Note: We all have different definitions of "family"—it may be blood relations, extended families-by-marriage, close friends who aren't related, or all of the above. In the interest of simplicity, this chapter will use "family" to describe any or all of the above, and to represent whatever may be your own definition of "family.")

We all look to our families for support and guidance during changing times, and today's workplace is constantly changing. It is essential that your family understands the new work realities if they are to provide you meaningful support. Without this understanding, they may not readily see the benefits of building the value of You.

Your family's input and insight are born of love and caring. They're on your side and want to protect you if they feel you are at risk. But if you don't take the time to communicate your views and objectives, you may get advice that you don't need. Family members may encourage you to "slow down a little," to forego volunteer work "until you have more time," or to reconsider your decision to enroll in evening or weekend classes. They may influence you to avoid any risks at the office, or cause you to second-guess your strengths or skills. Their motivation may be pure—but if they don't clearly understand your situation, their support can't be as effective as it might otherwise be.

There is no question that changing the way you work will have major effects on both yourself and your family. The process of finding work, working, volunteering and continuing your education can take its toll on relationships with spouses, children, extended family and friends. In recent years the equation for balancing self, work and family has become significantly more complicated and requires more effort than ever before. But by putting forth that effort, you can have a family that, in a real sense, works beside you as you strive to achieve your goals.

Most of that effort involves communication: honest, open, two-way communication. Your spouse and close friends must know your goals if they are to understand and support them. They need to understand where it is that you're headed and how you plan to get there. Clearly, it's up to you to explain your "mission" and vision for the future—in a way, to rally your own "troops" and enlist them in your cause.

Once your family understands, as you do, what it is that you're aiming for, they can quickly become some of your most valuable resources. Relatives and close friends may be extremely helpful as you create your list of personal strengths and skills. After all, they see you from their own unique perspectives and may, from the outside looking in, recognize strengths that you didn't. They can also, in many instances, point out areas in which you could use some improvement.

These people can also assist by helping you recall some of your past actions and results. They often remember things that have slipped your memory, or they may identify as results things that you did not. And just the knowledge that you have the support of your family can give you greater self-confidence and the strength to deal with inevitable stress.

Your network of friends and family may lead you to a volunteering opportunity—Elizabeth Taylor, a classic example, became a tireless worker for AIDS research because of the deaths of several of her friends and because her former daughter-in-law acquired the virus. A member of your "troops" may be interested in taking a class with you, or may agree to be your study partner.

I recently read about a man who was presented with a job opportunity offering significantly more money and better benefits than his current position, but it required that he become fluent in Spanish. So the man created a game in which he, his wife and their two sons, ages 9 and 11, all spent a summer learning Spanish. Even though the man worked longer hours that summer, his wife reported that in learning Spanish the family spent more time together than they had in any previous summer; and since the new job provided the man with a three-week paid vacation, they planned to celebrate their upcoming 16th anniversary on the beach in Mexico. Bravo for them!

We're all having to adapt to change much more rapidly than ever before, and it's human nature that where some see obstacles, others find opportunity. By openly discussing your plans and concerns with your family, you process your fears and anxieties in a healthy manner while you gain from the insight and experience of these people who know you so well. Suffering in isolation is not just unnecessary, but also akin to ignoring what can be one of your primary strengths: your family.

Friends and family members should not be seen as "burdens", but should be valued as willing cheerleaders, advisors, resources and people who share your successes as well as your uncertainties. It's easy to shut them out, assuming "they just wouldn't understand"—which, of course, they won't unless you *tell* them. You have to invest the time and effort to talk to them. You may not get the solution to every individual obstacle or problem, but over time your effort to communicate will pay dividends in ways you might never have expected.

Balancing Work, Family and Life: Making Entrepreneurship Work for You

In today's complex and demanding world, balancing work, family and the other demands of life can be difficult. Things can become unbearable when you have an inflexible job, boss or both. This is a major reason why people have begun to turn to entrepreneurial ventures to support their families: they want a better and more balanced lifestyle.

The biggest advantage is control. Literally working for yourself means you're in charge of your most precious resource: your time. Free from answering to bosses and abiding by someone else's rules, you can use that precious extra time instead for family and friends. It can enable you to live by a philosophy of not keeping the two spheres of your life—work and family—separate. As an employee, one of your most dreaded situations was probably the morning(s) you had to make an early call to your boss to say, "I can't come in; one of the kids is sick." As an entrepreneur, by contrast, you can tuck the ailing youngster into blankets on the sofa and make your client calls in between the taking of temperatures and the administering of grilled-cheese sandwiches. An entrepreneur can go to a friend's celebratory lunch and stay until the last laugh is enjoyed; an employee has to leave halfway through because he has only an hour for lunch.

Entrepreneurship does not, in itself, make your world perfect. But there are techniques you can use to make sure that your entrepreneurial venture is balanced with the other parts of your life.

Set Some Rules of Your Own

Although the self-employed You has more control over your life than the employee You would ever have, it's also easy to fall into the trap of letting work always come first at the expense of your family. Be diligent in guarding against this.

First, set up your office so you can make sure you're home for dinner—this can be one of the family's most important events of the day. If dinner with the family means going back to the office later to finish something up, the office's convenient location (the garage, the upstairs bedroom, the den) will make that quick and easy.

Second, limit your travel as much as possible. Make all efforts not to be out of town more than two or three nights a month, and turn your out-of-town client visits into day trips whenever possible. (This may take some juggling, but it can be done.)

Third, if you have children, don't shut them out of what you're doing. Show them your office. Explain that you're going to be working at home and you need their help too, because being at home doesn't mean you're always available; sometimes you'll need to close the door and concentrate. One working-at-home mom and her kids agreed that she will hang a red San Francisco 49ers pennant on her office door when she's doing something that can't be interrupted.

If your children are old enough, and if your work allows it, let them help: sticking stamps or labels on envelopes, stacking office supplies on shelves, even (if they're old enough, careful enough and interested enough) helping with the filing. Make them part of your work as much as possible—and appropriate—and they won't feel like they're competing with your work for your attention.

Get Some Help

Making a good life even better means coming to terms with an important fact: you, the entrepreneur—by definition, inclined to think you can do it all—must learn to delegate. This means giving other people tasks that don't absolutely require your attention. On the home front, for instance, maybe you'll hire a housekeeper to come in a couple of days a week for cleaning and perhaps some light cooking.

What *does* require your personal attention, in contrast, is tending to your children's needs, emotional and otherwise. This takes unpressured time, time when other demands are not distracting you, so you can listen to your children, respond appropriately and enjoy each other. (I know a home-office dad who hires someone to cover his phones every Wednesday from 1 to 4 p.m.; he and the children have a standing Wednesday "date" that may include sports, help with homework, a movie, or just hanging out together.)

Focus

This means staying in the present and focusing on what's in front of you. When you're on the job, be on the job. And when you're with the family, be with the family. Learn to live in and enjoy the present to make the best of your very good life.

Be Honest With Clients

Inevitably, a conflict will arise between a commitment to a client and the needs of your family. Don't hesitate to level with the client. Make sure that all special family events are marked on your business calendar so business deadlines and meeting dates won't clash. Check the calendar before you make a promise to a client. And when you accept a client's "rush" assignment, make sure the client knows that you're making an exception this time, that you can't (or won't) always be able to do so, and that you'll happily work with him to make sure realistic deadlines are set and met. (My local print shop has a sign over the desk that says, "Your Lack of Forethought Does Not Constitute My Emergency.")

Making the best of work and home life doesn't guarantee perfection. It only assures that the myriad and often conflicting ties in your life—work, spouse, children, friends—will loosen and flow more easily, one blending into another, rather than binding into a woefully unmanageable knot.

So set your own rules. Learn to delegate. Focus. Be honest. And pass this spirit on to your coworkers (if and when you have them). It's the entrepreneur's critical advantage. With control, you can create a workplace that's flexible and rewarding, and allows you to find balance in your life.

Chapter 7: Checkpoints for Learning

- It is essential that families understand the new work realities in order for them to provide you meaningful support and share in your successes. Without this understanding, they may not readily see the benefit of building the value of You.

- If you don't take the time to communicate your views and objectives, family and friends may offer advice (or worse, discouragement) that you don't need.

- The equation for balancing work, self, family and friends has become significantly more complicated, and requires more effort and two-way communication by you than ever before.

- Friends and family members should be seen by you as compatriots, collaborators, colleagues and willing resources during your challenging times, not as burdens.

• • • • •

Destiny is not a matter of chance,
it is a matter of choice; it is not a thing to be
waited for, it is a thing to be achieved.

—WILLIAM JENNINGS BRYAN

EIGHT

The Price of the New Value Paradigm

Freedom, it has been said, is never free. And it's true. As a society, we enjoy the freedom of a free market economy. With the exception of a few industries, no one tells us what is okay to buy or sell (assuming the transaction is lawful), or how much we should pay or charge for goods and services. This precept, above all others, is the foundation upon which our country has been built. It makes us the "land of opportunity" and is the primary attraction for millions of immigrants as they continue to come to America in search of its dream.

But with our free market comes a hefty price. Free markets are driven by competition. Competition means that some will win while others will lose. And inextricably entwined with our free market concept is the concept of *Caveat emptor*—"Let the buyer beware"—which means that to enjoy the benefits of a free market economy, consumers themselves must be responsible for their own actions. Government regulations and consumer protection laws may be there to help, but in the final analysis *it is up to you to protect yourself.*

Increased responsibility is often the price of freedom; rights are always accompanied by responsibilities. Americans have the right to "keep and bear arms," but must be responsible for the use of those arms. We are free to drink alcohol, but must demonstrate responsibility when out in public or when driving. And we have the right to speak our minds, unless we want to falsely yell "Fire!" in a crowded movie theatre. Freedom without responsibility, for certain, is anarchy—a state of total disorder.

Knowing your Value brings with it new freedom and independence. You no longer need be at the mercy of an employer when it comes to work security or opportunity for achievement. You can and must become dependent solely on yourself. If your Value is to be the basis for this independence, then clearly it is your responsibility to recognize, care for and grow that Value.

The world of business has been changed forever, and it will not change back. For people who have become value-minded, the new rules offer unlimited possibilities: the chance to succeed, freedom, independence, control. And with that new-found freedom come new responsibilities: responsibility for your own value, your relationships, your career and ultimately, your peace and prosperity and the wellbeing of your family.

If you really want security, you can no longer sit complacently as you blame others for your life's path, as if you are merely driftwood caught in the ebb and flow of the ocean's tide. Now that you've been told the truth, if you do not succeed in your endeavors there is clearly no one to blame but yourself. Pogo was right: "We have met the enemy and he is us."

Independence requires that if you are to find success, you must define your purpose and direction based largely on your skills, strengths and core tendencies, and then marshal all of your energy and resources toward achieving your goals. It takes continuous personal conviction, confidence and courage. It is never easy—but the rewards are immeasurable.

Once you understand and recognize your value, you need to take the time to communicate more frequently with the people around you—both on the job and in your personal life. You need to set more goals and do more planning if you are to achieve and maintain the balance that comes from the combination of your personal and working life. If you want prosperity, the bottom line is this: *you must design and effectively use your own compass, not simply latch onto someone else's.*

Having and exercising your freedoms has a price—always has, always will. But if you recognize the exciting opportunities found in the new environment, and you take full advantage of them, you will thrive in these changing times. If you don't, you won't.

Chapter 8: Checkpoints for Learning

- The new Value Paradigm means you no longer have to be at the mercy of your employer when it comes to your work security or your opportunities for achievement and growth.

- The world of business has been changed forever, and if you become *value-minded* you will find freedom, independence and control.

- With your freedom comes responsibility for your value, your relationships, your career and, ultimately, your peace and prosperity and the wellbeing of your family.

• • • • •

You have brains in your head.
You have feet in your shoes.
You can steer yourself
any direction you choose.

—THEODOR SEUSS GEISEL (DR. SEUSS)

NINE

The Challenge: Your Future Is Now

Now that you've finished this book, you have the information and tools to change your professional (and personal) life.

Among other things, this book challenges you to:

- Know that your Value is comprised of your *strengths*, the *actions* you take to demonstrate those strengths, and the specific *results* you have produced by applying your strengths

- Be prepared to communicate your Value, in specifics, on demand

- Realize that You are the product, and that your product must constantly be improved to keep it marketable and competitive

- Appreciate that when you face challenges, you need to see your friends, family and colleagues as part of your solution rather than the problem

- Create your personal vision, plan it and then take the necessary steps to achieve it; and

- Savor and preserve the freedom and control that result from knowing your Value, developing your Value, and finding further opportunities to invest it

It is you, and you alone, who will determine your Value and market that value—to the many "buyers" that will happily benefit from your contributions and support.

It has been said that you can't change what you don't face. So when will you begin? Tomorrow? The next day? Maybe on New Year's Day, St. Patrick's Day, your birthday? The best answer is, "Today. Right now. This minute."

We all tend to put off what seems too challenging. And once it's postponed, any task seems less important. After a while, we can't even remember what "it" was or why we were so interested in doing it.

Don't fall into that trap this time. Your career—and your life—are far too important. Take action today... and every single day. Learn—and constantly build your value.

Your future—a new, better, more secure future— begins this very instant. Today more than ever before, you are your own "boss". It's entirely up to you whether or not you are working for a good employer.

Onward!

• • • • •

APPENDIX

Checkpoints for Learning: Summary

CHAPTER 1: THE WORKPLACE: MY, HOW YOU'VE CHANGED

Checkpoints for Learning:

- Today, you are hired and retained on the basis of your demonstrated self-reliance and your proven track record of contributing results.

- Successful leaders of the new millennium are more "empowering" than powerful—they rely on their own competence rather than mere authority to get the job done, and they expect you to do the same.

- Work security has shifted from being something dictated by an employer to something largely controlled by you. "At will" employment has become a two-way street. Properly self-managed, your side of that street will provide you a long and successful career.

- You must understand your own Value and be able to communicate and demonstrate your worth on demand. Facing the reality that you, and not others, are responsible for your life and career sets you free to take greater responsibility for shaping your own future.

- By understanding the scope and types of changes that have occurred in the workplace, you can take full advantage of the opportunities available to you by knowing that by performing you can control your own work security and career.

Chapter 2: First Steps

Checkpoints for Learning:

- All of the insight you need to thrive in today's changed workplace is entirely learnable and, like riding a bicycle, once learned, you'll never forget it.

- Both today and in the future, being hired and retained depends on the specific results you contribute, not merely your regular attendance, positive attitude or formal education.

- Whatever security "jobs" may have offered in the past is now being far outweighed by their limitations on your opportunities to learn and use new skills by making broader contributions "outside the box".

- To succeed, you need to know exactly what your basic skills are and, likewise, you must be conscious of your weaknesses.
- Your educational background, past experience or even skills alone won't sell your "product". Your features and benefits, in the form of results that you have and will consistently attain, will.
- Keeping your current skills up to date, along with acquiring new ones that produce the results you sell, is the process you must become comfortable with if you are to be continuously investment-worthy and thus "employed".

CHAPTER 3: THE VALUE FORMULA

Checkpoints for Learning:

Some basic principles for achieving more career self-reliance and control over your working future include the following:

- To be a successful self-employed businessperson, you need to understand that you are your own "product".
- You need to know your product's unique features and benefits—your skills, strengths, achievements, qualities and attributes.
- You need to toot your own horn at job interviews and performance evaluations—present the facts about your performance and let them speak to your value.

- The Value Formula: Strengths + Actions + Results = Your Value

- Your strengths and skills are the things at which you excel.

- Your actions are the things that you do which demonstrate or apply your strengths.

- Results are the bottom line of every business venture, including yours.

- If you like what you do, you will be much better at it than if you don't like what you do.

- Know which category best describes yourself and your coworkers:
  - Humanist
  - Organizer
  - Energizer
  - Futurist

- Well thought out goals and an action/business plan to meet your goals are important steps in controlling your career.

CHAPTER 5: KAIZEN: CONTINUOUSLY BUILDING YOUR VALUE FOR LONG-TERM SUCCESS

Checkpoints for Learning:

- The Japanese business-related concept Kaizen is defined as "continuous quality improvement," which can be applied to your own product: You.

- Some keys to continuous quality improvement include:

- Learning to want to learn
- Volunteering

• Volunteering can result in building your inventory of accomplishments that can enhance your current work security and future employability.

• In today's workplace You are the product and, like any product, you must continuously strive to improve yourself—as you do through volunteering and continuing education.

• Quality, like value, requires personal commitment, and thus is an "inside job."

CHAPTER 6: PERSONAL MASTERY: CONTROLLING YOUR OWN FUTURE

Checkpoints for Learning:

• Personal mastery means continually expanding yourself and your abilities to achieve the results you want in your life.

• "Creative tension" is the gap between where you are and where you want to be. That "tension" needs to be strong enough to cause you to act, yet not so strong that you see no hope of achieving your goals and give up.

• People who have achieved personal mastery:
- find purpose in their lives
- welcome change
- are inquisitive
- feel connected to themselves as well as others
- see life as a challenging journey, and, most importantly, *choose to be proactive participants in that journey.*

- Personal mastery starts with seeing yourself as an individual who is able to cope with life's challenges—but even more, it means taking full responsibility for creating your personal vision and then *making it happen.*

CHAPTER 7: FAMILY MATTERS

Checkpoints for Learning:

- It is essential that families understand the new work realities in order for them to provide you meaningful support and share in your successes. Without this understanding, they may not readily see the benefit of building the value of You.

- If you don't take the time to communicate your views and objectives, family and friends may offer advice (or worse, discouragement) that you don't need.

- The equation for balancing work, self, family and friends has become significantly more complicated, and requires more effort and two-way communication by you than ever before.

- Friends and family members should be seen by you as compatriots, collaborators, colleagues and willing resources during your challenging times, not as burdens.

CHAPTER 8: THE PRICE OF THE NEW VALUE PARADIGM

Checkpoints for Learning:

- The new Value Paradigm means you no longer have to be at the mercy of your employer when it comes to your work security or your opportunities for achievement and growth.

- The world of business has been changed forever, and if you become *value-minded* you will find freedom, independence and control.
- With your freedom comes responsibility for your value, your relationships, your career and, ultimately, your peace and prosperity, and the wellbeing of your family.

ABOUT THE AUTHOR

Author P. Anthony (Tony) Burnham, Esq., has spent a lifetime working in and observing both American and international business. His strong entrepreneurial spirit, combined with over three decades of preventive labor and employment law, senior corporate human resources management and organizational development experience has given him a unique and valuable perspective on today's results-focused and transitional workplace.

For 17 years, Tony served as Labor and Employment Counsel for the Los Angeles–based Fortune 100 Carnation Company, successfully managing the company's legal risks through the 1970s and early '80s when labor relations, employment discrimination and "wrongful" discharge issues and claims exposed the firm to significant federal and state liability. He was also involved in the company's international operations, including consolidations, plant closures and ensuring senior executive accountability throughout Europe.

After Carnation was acquired by the Switzerland-based Nestlé company in 1985, the new president and CEO of the combined companies asked Tony to establish a corporate Human Resources Management function for the multibillion-dollar organization. As Nestlé/Carnation's Corporate Vice President of Human Resources Management, Tony created "partnering" and "win-win" relationships between the company and its multinational workforce. He developed and implemented company-wide HR policies that emphasized and valued individual performance by giving employees incentives to produce more, better, faster and cheaper results.

Under Tony's leadership, the company successfully changed from a top-down management style that emphasized seniority to a collaborative structure that valued results. Driven by this new philosophy, the company was able to both reduce the size of its workforce and increase profitability.

After leaving Nestlé/Carnation, Tony co-founded the ProACTIVE Institute, of Newport Beach, California, in early 1992. Growing out of Tony's success in change management at Nestlé/Carnation, the Institute advised employers on organizational transition and specialized in results-focused career development training for their employees.

ProACTIVE Institute taught employability skills. It successfully trained thousands of blue- and white-collar employees how to define, quantify and effectively communicate their unique value to their current and future employers.

In 1997 Tony returned to the active practice of employment law. He was invited to become "of counsel" to the Newport Beach office of Fisher & Phillips LLP, a national law firm. Since 1943, F&P has exclusively practiced labor and employment law, representing only management. Tony helped develop F&P's creative approach to "preventive" employment law. His practice continued to emphasize the importance of adopting the "best" employment practices which helped clients avoid employee related disputes altogether, and increased the productivity and commitment of each client's valued employees.

Tony then turned to the emerging human capital management industry, serving as Executive Vice President and Employment Counsel with the Abbott Resource Group, Inc., of Irvine, Calif. This 30-year-old firm provides contingent staffing and alternative workforce solutions to support rapidly growing businesses.

Today, Tony is a co-founder, President and Employment Counsel of the Human Capital Co-Op, LLC (HCC), located in Mission Viejo, California. HCC provides cost-effective, "Fortune 50" level employment counsel and human resources solutions to small and mid-sized businesses by means of a monthly subscription. Subscribing businesses access HCC's services either directly from HCC or by referral to HCC from a "trusted advisor", such as an insurance broker, accountant or attorney. These "trusted advisors" become members of HCC's "cooperative" in order to provide their clients with the highest available level of human capital management expertise at a cost affordable to a smaller business.

Tony's work continues to emphasize the need for businesses to attract, hire, engage and value workers who are passionate about achieving results both for themselves and for their employers. He has learned from 35 years of experience as a lawyer, litigator, executive and entrepreneur that a business driven by the enlightened self-interest of its results-focused people will be able to both obtain and maintain a critical competitive edge, especially in today's fast-paced and constantly changing "new" economy. For those achievers and the fortunate businesses to which they choose to contribute, he has written *Employed for Life!*